THE WORLD'S GREATEST
MOTORBIKES

Ian Graham

Raintree

Chicago, Illinois

Customer Service 888-363-4266
Visit our website at
www.heinemannraintree.com

For more information address the publisher:
Raintree, 100 N. LaSalle, Suite 1200, Chicago,
IL 60602

Editorial: Andrew Farrow and Dan Nunn
Design: Ron Kamen and Philippa Baile
Picture Research: Hannah Taylor and Elaine
 Willis
Production: Duncan Gilbert

Originated by Dot Gradations Ltd.
Printed in China

The paper used to print this book comes from
sustainable resources.

10 09 08 07 06
10 9 8 7 6 5 4 3 2 1

**Library of Congress Cataloging-in-
Publication Data**
Graham, Ian, 1953-
  Motorbikes / Ian Graham.
    p. cm. -- (The world's greatest)
  Includes bibliographical references and
  index.
  ISBN 1-4109-2084-4 (library binding-
  hardcover) -- ISBN 1-4109-2091-7 (pbk.)
  1. Mopeds--Juvenile literature.
  I. Title. II. Series.
  TL443.G73 2005
  629.227'5--dc22
                          2005016393

Acknowledgments
The publishers would like to thank the
following for permission to reproduce
photographs:

American Suzuki Motor Corporation pp. **6**, **7
top**, **7 bottom**, **8 bottom**; Associated Press
pp. **21**, **24 bottom**; Cagivausa p. **19**; Corbis
pp. **5** (Bettmann), **14** (Reuters/Michael
Kooren), **24 top** (Bettmann); Daimler Chrysler
p. **25**; Dave Campos p. **22**; Ducati pp. **10**, **11**;
Getty Images pp. **4** (AFP/Jim Watson), **16**
(Allsport/Mike Cooper), **17** (Allsport/Mike
Cooper), **18** (AFP/Dimitar Dilkoff), **20**
(Jonathan Ferry); Honda pp. **8 top**, **9**;
Landracing.com p. **23**; Ronald Grant Archive
p. **13 bottom**; The Car Photo Library pp. **12**
(David Kimber), **13 top** (David Kimber);
Yamaha pp. **1**, **15**.

Cover photograph of Valentino Rossi on his
Honda Moto GP bike, October 2003, reproduced
with permission of Corbis/Reuters/Heino Kalis.

Every effort has been made to contact
copyright holders of any material reproduced
in this book. Any omissions will be rectified in
subsequent printings if notice is given to the
publishers.

Contents

Some words are shown in bold, **like this.** You can find out what they mean by looking in the glossary.

Motorbikes

There are many kinds of motorbikes. Millions of people all over the world ride them.

Types of motorbikes

Some motorbikes are for riding on roads. Motorbikes called **cruisers** and **tourers** are comfortable for long journeys. **Sports bikes** are more fun and exciting to ride, but they are not as comfortable. Other bikes are for riding off the road and for racing. Motocross bikes are tall, light bikes for bumpy, muddy ground. Racing bikes are built to go very fast on a special racetrack.

Motorbikes today have two wheels and an engine in the middle, just like the Daimler Einspur (see right). But modern bikes are stronger and more powerful. They are also easier to ride and have better brakes.

When did it all begin?

The first motorbike was built in Germany by Gottlieb Daimler in 1885. Daimler made a wooden bicycle and added a small gasoline engine. The bike was called the Einspur.

Motorbikes have changed a lot since the Einspur. Compare Daimler's motorbike with a modern one like the Honda Fireblade!

Daimler's Einspur motorbike was ridden for the first time by his son Paul on November 10, 1885.

 **Daimler Einspur**	**Honda CBR1000RR Fireblade**
Built in: **1885**	**2005**
Engine: **16 cu. in./265 cc**	**61 cu. in./998 cc**
Power: **0.5 horsepower**	**170 horsepower**
Top speed: **8 mph/12 kph**	**178 mph/286 kph**

The Fastest Road Bike

The world's fastest road bike is the Suzuki GSX1300R Hayabusa. It has a powerful engine. But a powerful engine is not enough to make a motorbike go really fast. The reason the Hayabusa can go so fast is because it has a really smooth shape.

Beating drag

When a motorbike moves, it goes through the air. The air pushes back and slows it down. The push of the air against the bike is called **drag**. Some shapes make a lot of drag. The smooth shape of the Hayabusa means the drag is very small. This makes it go very fast.

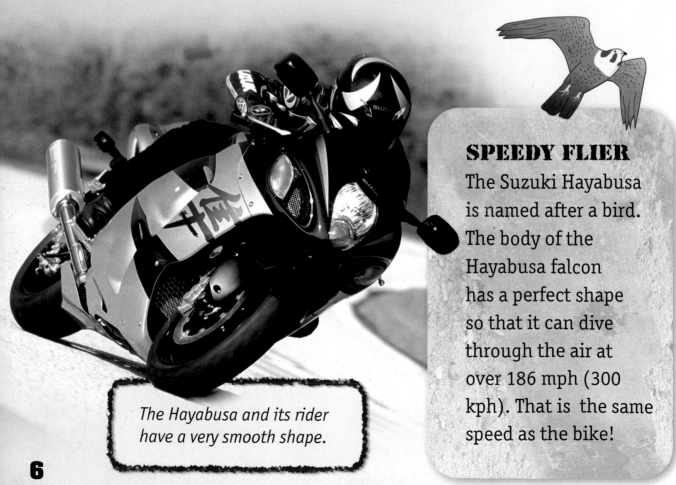

SPEEDY FLIER

The Suzuki Hayabusa is named after a bird. The body of the Hayabusa falcon has a perfect shape so that it can dive through the air at over 186 mph (300 kph). That is the same speed as the bike!

The Hayabusa and its rider have a very smooth shape.

Suzuki GSX1300R Hayabusa

Engine:	**79 cu. in./1,299 cc**
Power:	**173 horsepower**
Weight:	**478 lb./217 kg**
Top Speed:	**194 mph/312 kph**

The wedge-shaped nose slices easily through the air at high speed.

A motorbike engine needs air to burn its fuel. Holes on each side of the Hayabusa's nose let lots of air flow to the engine.

Other Fast Road Bikes

There are many fast motorbikes for the road. They are called sports road bikes. The fastest include the Honda Fireblade, the Honda Super Blackbird, and the Suzuki GSX-R1000.

Black beauty

The Honda Super Blackbird was once the fastest road motorbike. Its engine is as big as some car engines. The Super Blackbird is bigger and heavier than other sports road bikes. It is also more comfortable to ride.

The Super Blackbird is still one of the world's fastest motorbikes.

The Suzuki GSX-R1000 is very light for its size, so it is very fast, too.

Fast Fireblade

The Honda Fireblade is one of the most popular sports road bikes today. It is lighter than other road bikes the same size. This helps to make it faster. It also makes it more exciting to ride. The Fireblade has been changed over the years to keep it up to date. Today, it has a bigger and more powerful engine.

> The latest Honda Fireblade has a bigger engine than the first Fireblade, and it goes faster.

	Honda Super Blackbird	**Honda Fireblade**
Engine:	69 cu. in./1,137 cc	61 cu. in./998 cc
Power:	150 horsepower	170 horsepower
Weight:	500 lb./227 kg	395 lb./179 kg
Top Speed:	186 mph/300 kph	178 mph/286 kph

The Most Wanted Road Bike

The Ducati 999R is a road bike that lots of people would like to ride. They would like to ride the racing version, too!

Superbike!

Ducati bikes are famous for being beautiful and fast. They have been very successful in **Superbike** racing. The Ducati used in Superbike racing today is the Ducati 999F05. It is the racing version of the Ducati 999R road bike. To make the racing bike, nearly every part of the road bike was slimmed down or made from a different material to make it lighter.

The Ducati 999's streamlined shape was designed by computers. The bike in this photo is the Superbike racing version.

NEAT NOSE

One of the lights at the front of the Ducati 999R is above the other. This makes the bike's nose narrower, so it cuts through the air better at high speeds.

A Ducati 999R road bike leans over to take a turn at high speed.

	Ducati 999R	**Ducati 999F05**
Type of Bike:	**Road bike**	**Superbike racer**
Engine:	**61 cu. in./999 cc**	**61 cu. in./999 cc**
Power:	**150 horsepower**	**194 horsepower**
Weight:	**423 lb./192 kg**	**364 lb./165 kg**
Top Speed:	**170 mph/275 kph**	**186 mph/300 kph**

The Coolest Motorbike

There are fashions in motorbikes just like fashions in clothes and music. Some motorbikes are *cooler* than others. Many people think the coolest motorbikes are Harley-Davidsons. They are often called Harleys or hogs.

Classic styling

Harley-Davidson has been making motorbikes for more than 100 years. Unlike other motorbike makers, it has kept the same style. Today, the classic Harley-Davidson style is cooler and more popular than ever. One of the bestselling Harleys is the Road King. It is a very comfortable bike for riding long distances.

Harley-Davidson Road King

Engine:	**88 cu. in./1,449 cc**
Weight:	**732 lb./332 kg**
Length:	**8 ft./2.4 m**
Wheelbase:	**5 ft. 3 in./1.6 m**

The Road King is a very comfortable bike for riding long distances. Cruisers like the Road King are longer and heavier than sports bikes.

Potato engine

Harleys have an engine called a **V-twin**. It is called this because the **fuel** is burned in two **cylinders** joined at the bottom to make a V shape. If you want to know what a big V-twin Harley engine sounds like, just say *potato-potato-potato-potato!*

The Harley-Davidson Electra Glide is one of the best-equipped touring bikes there is. It has its own stereo music system. It also has an intercom to let the rider and passenger talk to each other.

Harley owners often make their bikes look different from everyone else's. This is called customizing. The most famous type of customized Harley was the 1970s chopper. The chopper had long handlebars called ape-hangers!

The Fastest Racing Bikes

The fastest and most exciting motorbike races are **MotoGP** races. Bikes are made especially for MotoGP racing. These races take place all over the world.

Turning on the power

MotoGP rules say the bikes can have 990 cc (60 cu. in.) engines. These engines are very powerful. A MotoGP bike like the Yamaha YZR-M1 can reach over 200 mph (322 kph).

MotoGP riders lean their bikes over to steer them around a turn. The tires have to grip the track even at these crazy angles.

Yamaha YZR-M1 MotoGP Race Bike

Engine: **60 cu. in./990 cc**
Power: **240 horsepower**
Top Speed: **Over 200 mph/322 kph**

Staying on track

A rider has to use his engine's power carefully. A bike will spin and tumble off the track if the rider goes too fast around a turn or **accelerates** too quickly.

windshield

fairing

The Yamaha YZR-M1 is one of the best MotoGP racing bikes. In this photo, the rider is tucked in behind the **fairing** *and windshield. This helps air to flow smoothly over the bike and rider.*

Sidecar Racers

Some road bikes carry an extra passenger in a **sidecar**. The sidecar looks like a seat with a wheel. People often race motorbikes and sidecars. Road bikes and sidecars are made separately and then joined. A racing bike and sidecar are made together as one vehicle. The motorbike and front of the sidecar have a **streamlined** body called a fairing.

The rider and passenger crouch down behind the motorbike and sidecar body as they speed along a straight part of the track.

Staying upright

A motorbike leans over to help it turn. But a motorbike with a sidecar cannot lean over. It has to stay upright. The passenger in a racing sidecar leans over as far as possible toward the inside of each turn. This stops the bike from toppling over. It also lets the bike take turns faster.

Flat-top tires

Racing sidecars have tires that are very wide and flat. This produces the most grip so that they can go around turns faster.

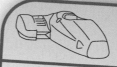

Sidecar Racer

Length:	8 ft. 10 in./2.7 m
Height:	2 ft. 6 in./75 cm
Weight:	825 lb./375 kg
Engine:	61 cu. in./1,000 cc
Power:	180 horsepower
Top Speed:	175 mph/280 kph

As the motorbike turns, the passenger leans toward the inside of the turn to balance the bike.

Motocross Bikes

Motocross is motorbike racing in mud! The bikes race around a bumpy, muddy course. Motocross bikes are specially made for the bumps and mud.

Built for bumps

A motocross bike has to be very strong. Its engine is higher above the ground to stop it hitting bumps. That makes motocross bikes like the Husqvarna TC450 taller than other bikes. A road bike like the Kawasaki ZX-10R is much lower. It would scrape along the bumps.

Motocross courses include hills and jumps that send the bikes flying into the air.

	Husqvarna TC450 Motocross Bike 	Kawasaki ZX-10R Road Bike
Engine:	27 cu. in./449 cc	61 cu. in./998 cc
Weight:	231 lb./105 kg	375 lb./170 kg
Seat Height:	3 ft. 2 in./97 cm	2 ft. 8 in./82.5 cm
Total Height:	4 ft. 2 in./128 cm	3 ft. 8 in./111.5 cm

4 ft. 2 in./ 128 cm

Springy wheels

Like all motorbikes, the engine in a motocross bike drives the back wheel. The back wheel has to stay on the ground to keep the bike going. A big spring under the seat presses the wheel down. The wheel can move up and down a long way. This allows it to follow all the humps and hollows in the ground.

The Husqvarna TC450 is a motocross bike. It has knobby tires. These dig into soft, muddy ground and grip better.

The Most Powerful Racing Bike

The most powerful racing bikes are **drag bikes**. Drag bikes do not race around and around a circuit. They race along a straight track, two bikes at a time.

Drag bikes are designed to go as fast as possible in a straight line. They are long and low, with very powerful engines. The fastest and most powerful are the Top Fuel bikes. They can reach a speed of more than 220 mph (350 kph) in just over six seconds!

A rider spins the bike's back wheel before a race to heat it up. A hot tire grips the track better.

Getting a grip

Drag bikes have a big, wide back tire. The engine drives the back wheel. The big tire helps to grip the track better. Better grip means faster acceleration. The bike that can accelerate the fastest, crosses the finish line first.

FLYING START

The fastest drag bikes accelerate more than three times faster than most sports cars.

Top Fuel Drag Bike

Engine:	168 cu. in./2,750 cc
Power:	up to 1,000 horsepower
Top Speed:	220 mph/350 kph
Wheelbase:	7 ft. 6 in./2.3 m

A drag bike has a long bar called a wheelie bar at the back. This stops the bike rearing up. It also stops the bike from flipping over backward as it accelerates.

The Fastest Motorbikes on Earth

On Saturday, July, 14, 1990, Dave Campos started the engine of his strange-looking motorbike. He set a new **land speed record** for motorbikes of 322 mph (518 kph).

Easyriders

The motorbike was called Easyriders. It looks like a long black tube. The rider must lie down on his or her back inside a closed cockpit. The rider cannot use the feet to steady the bike. Metal feet stick out to hold it upright. It is powered by two Harley-Davidson motorbike engines.

Motorbikes like Easyriders, shaped like long tubes, are called **streamliners**.

HEAVYWEIGHT MACHINE
Easyriders weighs more than five road bikes like the Suzuki Hayabusa.

Fastest ever

The highest speed ever reached by a motorbike is thought to be 370 mph (595 kph). The Feuling Advanced Technologies motorbike reached this speed in 1997.

Getting started

The world's fastest motorbikes are designed to run best at top speed. Their engines do not work very well going slowly. In fact, the bike has to be traveling at about 80 mph (130 kph) before the engine will even start! To get around this, a car or truck tows the bike up to its starting speed.

The Feuling Advanced Technologies motorbike is probably the world's fastest motorcycle.

	Easyriders Land Speed Record Bike	Suzuki Hayabusa Road Bike
Length:	23 ft./7 m	7 ft./2.14 m
Engine:	182 cu. in./3,000 cc	79 cu. in./1,299 cc
Weight:	2,500 lb./1,135 kg	478 lb./217 kg
Top Speed:	322 mph/518 kph	194 mph/312 kph

Other Extreme Bikes

Before Dave Campos set the land speed record for motorbikes in 1990, the record had been held for 12 years by Don Vesco. The motorbike used was called Lightning Bolt.

Changing name

Lightning Bolt started as a different motorbike! It had held another land speed record and was called Silver Bird. To go even faster, it needed new engines. The new engines were bigger. Silver Bird was made longer to fit them in. The longer motorbike with its new engines was given a new name—Lightning Bolt.

Don Vesco set a land speed record of 318 mph (512 kph) with a motorbike called Lightning Bolt in 1978.

Lightning Bolt was built from another motorbike, called Silver Bird. This set a land speed record of 302 mph (487 kph) in 1975.

The Dodge Tomahawk is a four-wheel monster motorbike with a car engine!

Riding the Tomahawk

The Dodge Tomahawk is almost as fast as a land speed record motorbike. It is a concept vehicle. This means that it has been built to show what is possible, but it may not be made in large numbers. Its huge engine usually powers a Dodge Viper supercar. To make it steadier, it has two wheels at the front and two at the back.

SUPERBIKE

A Dodge Tomahawk could go faster than a Formula 1 racing car! However, it would be too difficult to ride at that speed.

	Dodge Tomahawk	Lightning Bolt
Type:	Concept vehicle	Land speed record bike
Engine:	505 cu. in./8,277 cc	124 cu. in./2,026 cc
Power:	500 horsepower	300 horsepower
Top Speed:	300 mph/480 kph	318 mph/513 kph

Facts and Figures

There are hundreds of types of motorbike. Some of the world's top bikes are listed here. You can use the information to see which is the most powerful or the fastest.

If you want to find out more, read the section called Further Information on pages 30 and 31.

Historic Motorbikes	Date	Engine	Power	Top Speed
Daimler Einspur (Germany)	1885	16 cu. in./265 cc	0.5 horsepower	8 mph/12 kph
Indian Powerplus (USA)	1918	61 cu. in./998 cc	18 horsepower	60 mph/96 kph
Harley-Davidson WL45 (USA)	1949	45 cu. in./742 cc	25 horsepower	75 mph/120 kph
Triumph Bonneville (UK)	1959	40 cu. in./649 cc	46 horsepower	110 mph/177 kph

Road Bikes	Weight	Engine	Power	Top Speed
Ducati 999R (Italy)	423 lb./192 kg	61 cu. in./999 cc	150 horsepower	178 mph/286 kph
Harley-Davidson Road King (USA)	732 lb./332 kg	88 cu. in./1,449 cc	66 horsepower	103 mph/166 kph
Honda CBR1000RR Fireblade (Japan)	395 lb./179 kg	61 cu. in./998 cc	170 horsepower	178 mph/286 kph
Honda CBR1100XX Super Blackbird (Japan)	500 lb./227 kg	69 cu. in./1,137 cc	150 horsepower	186 mph/300 kph
Kawasaki ZX-10R (Japan)	375 lb./170 kg	61 cu. in./998 cc	181 horsepower	186 mph/300 kph
Suzuki GSX1300R Hayabusa (Japan)	478 lb./217 kg	79 cu. in./1,299 cc	173 horsepower	194 mph/312 kph

Racing Bikes	Championship	Engine	Power	Top Speed *
Ducati Desmosedici (Italy)	MotoGP	60 cu. in./989 cc	220 horsepower	202 mph/325 kph
Honda RC211V (Japan)	MotoGP	60 cu. in./990 cc	240 horsepower	202 mph/325 kph
Yamaha YZR-M1 (Japan)	MotoGP	60 cu. in./990 cc	240 horsepower	202 mph/325 kph
Ducati 999RS F05 (Italy)	Superbike	61 cu. in./999 cc	194 horsepower	194 mph/312 kph
Honda CBR1000RR (Japan)	Superbike	61 cu. in./998 cc	210 horsepower	194 mph/312 kph
Suzuki GSX-R1000 (Japan)	Superbike	61 cu. in./998 cc	207 horsepower	194 mph/312 kph
Husqvarna TC450 (Sweden)	Motocross	27 cu. in./449 cc	59 horsepower	Not known

* In the hands of top riders, some of these bikes may reach even higher speeds.

Drag Bikes	Wheelbase	Engine	Power	Top Speed
Top Fuel Drag Bike (USA)	7 ft. 6 in./2.3 m	168 cu. in./2,750 cc/	1,000 horsepower	220 mph/350 kph
Pro Stock Drag Bike (USA)	5 ft. 10 in./1.8 m	91 cu. in./1,500 cc	300 horsepower	200 mph/320 kph

Land Speed Record Bikes	Weight	Engine	Power	Top Speed
Easyriders (USA)	2,500 lb./1,135 kg	182 cu. in./3,000 cc	Not known	322 mph/518 kph
Lightning Bolt (USA)	Not known	124 cu. in./2,026 cc	300 horsepower	318 mph/513 kph

Concept Bikes	Weight	Engine	Power	Top Speed
Dodge Tomahawk (USA)	1,500 lb./680 kg	505 cu. in./8,277 cc	500 horsepower	300 mph/480 kph

The land speed record

The first motorbike speed record of 75.9 mph (122.14 kph) was set in 1909 by William Cook on a Peugeot NLG. By 1920, motorbikes were going faster than 100 mph (160 kph). The record passed 200 mph (320 kph) in the 1950s. By then, torpedo-shaped motorbikes called streamliners were being used. They took the record above 300 mph (480 kph) in the 1970s. Today, the record stands at 322.1 mph (518.4 kph).

Motorbike engines

Motorbike engines work like car engines. Fuel burns inside tube-shaped cylinders. This makes metal drums called pistons go up and down. The up and down movements are changed into a turning motion that drives the back wheel. The smallest motorbike engines have only one cylinder. A popular type of engine is the V-twin. It has two cylinders joined at the bottom to form a V shape. Other bikes have in-line engines—the cylinders are in a straight line. An in-line four engine has four cylinders in a line.

Glossary

accelerate go faster

cc cubic centimeter. A space that is one centimeter long, high, and wide. The space inside an engine where the fuel is burned is measured in cc (say *see-sees*). The smallest motorbikes have engines of about 50 cc. The biggest road bike engine is 2,300 cc, on the Triumph Rocket III.

cruiser type of motorbike that is built more for comfort and looks than speed and performance

cu. in. cubic inch. A space that is one inch long, high, and wide. The space inside an engine where the fuel is burned is measured in cubic inches (cu. in.). The smallest motorbikes have engines of about 3 cu. in. The biggest road bikes have 140 cu. in. engines.

cylinder part of an engine shaped like a tube. The fuel is burned here. Most motorbike engines have one, two, or four cylinders.

drag slowing effect of the air. When something tries to move through air, the air pushes back and slows it down. Some shapes cause more drag than others.

drag bike motorbike designed to go as fast as possible in a straight line

fairing a smooth cover around a motorbike. A fairing gives a bike a smoother shape so that it can slip through the air faster.

fuel substance that is burned inside a motorbike engine. Most motorbikes burn gasoline. A few racing motorbikes burn special fuels that produce more power.

horsepower the power of an engine. A small motorbike might have an engine of less than 10 horsepower. A medium-sized motorbike has an engine of about 50–60 horsepower. The biggest and fastest bikes have engines of more than 150 horsepower. The most powerful drag bikes can have 1,000 horsepower engines.

land speed record the fastest speed reached by a vehicle on land. The time a motorbike takes to go along a straight course and come back again is measured. The time is used to work out the motorbike's speed.

MotoGP the leading world motorbike racing championship

sidecar passenger seat fixed to the side of a motorbike. Specially built motorbikes and sidecars take part in races.

sports bike motorbike that is built for its speed and sport-like performance

streamlined the right shape to slip through the air easily. Fast motorbikes have a streamlined shape so that air flows around them smoothly and does not slow them down.

streamliner special type of motorbike shaped like a long thin tube. Streamliners are used to set the fastest speed records.

Superbike type of racing motorbike. Superbikes are similar to ordinary bikes that people can own.

tourer type of motorbike that is built for making long journeys. It has room for a passenger and luggage.

V-twin common type of motorbike engine. A V-twin has two cylinders joined at the bottom to make a V shape.

Further Information

You can find out more information about motorbikes and motorbike racing by reading the following books about the subject.

Books to read

Graham, Ian. *Superbikes: Designed for Success*. Chicago: Heinemann Library, 2003.

Ryan, Ray and Bill Forsyth and Jeremy Holland. *Motocross Racers: 30 Years of Legendary Dirt Bikes*. Osceola, WI: Motorbooks International, 2003.

Sievert, Terri. *Motocross Racing (Edge Books)*. Mankato, MN: Capstone Press, 2004.

Christopher, Matthew F. *Dirt Bike Racer*. New York: Little, Brown, 1986.

Places to visit

Motorcycle Hall of Fame Museum

Located in Pickerington, Ohio, this musuem features several exhibits, including Motocross America, the Hall of Fame Gallery, and the Founders Hall. Visitors can experience motocross from its start in the 1920s to today, and discover how its technology and popularity have changed with time. The gallery features many famous racing cycles.

National Motorcycle Museum

The National Motorcycle Museum's Hall of Fame is located in Anamosa, Iowa. This museum displays a wall of engines, a motorbike service store from the early 1900s, and several hillclimbers. Other exhibits include vintage motorbikes, racing bikes, and photographs.

Index